Family Intent
The Ultimate Betrayal

by

Randolph Blake

authorHOUSE™

1663 LIBERTY DRIVE, SUITE 200
BLOOMINGTON, INDIANA 47403
(800) 839-8640
WWW.AUTHORHOUSE.COM

First published by AuthorHouse 08/11/05

ISBN: 1-4208-5657-X (e)
ISBN: 1-4208-5656-1 (sc)

Library of Congress Control Number: 2005904182

Printed in the United States of America
Bloomington, Indiana

This book is printed on acid-free paper.

<u>Preface:</u>

Trapped in a nightmare within a nightmare,

Blake finds himself trying to cope with the

Void of his beloved wife and precious

Daughter.

His family, stolen from him with malicious

Intent.

He is now poised on the edge of reality and

Insanity.

Reflecting in the mirror image deep within his soul, he

senses the *void*.

--It would soon be here to claim him.

The *"Escape"* beckons

DEDICATION:

This book is dedicated to the family and friends who have helped carry me through these troubled times. To my mother and father for instilling in me our family heritage and values, I love and cherish you both dearly. To my closest friends, who have lived and experienced this story. Thank you for your support and understanding. In addition, to all who have encouraged me through the years to write this story, my deepest respect. Moreover, foremost to my precious daughter for with out your love and compassion, this story may have never been told. I love you most.   -- Daddy.

<u>Chapter One</u>

"The Escape"

It is happening again, the same nightmare over and over. Each and every night sleep was refused, denied, no -- stolen! No matter how hard he tried, every night bred the same relentless betrayal. Gone! They were gone -- stolen. Awakened now by the cold sweat that ran from his brow, Blake's heart pounded as though it would erupt from the very place that once held an inexhaustible supply of the very essence that held the bond of children, family, and lovers together.

The sheets now soaked again with the frustration of unforgiving vivid memories so real that even after years of failed relationships, it felt as though it had happened only yesterday. Before his family -- was stolen. Shaking uncontrollably, Blake managed to gather his composure. Knowing it would only be a matter of time, before the episode or saga would be re-lived again. The bathroom tile was cold, hard on the soles of his feet as he staggered weak, towards the bathroom sink. He must reach it! Must see himself, remember who he was.

The coldness was in its own way familiar almost comforting. Yet he knew it was shaded. That feeling now sent shivers cascading up his legs, back and arms. He must not lose control again! He must not retreat to the -- "Escape" that place where all is lost. Hope is abandoned and the essence of your very soul is lost in the void. It had claimed everything that he was, had become and possibly would ever be. Now in the mirror his own eyes revealed the façade that he himself knew he hid behind. "For the eyes are the windows to the soul," they say. In addition, his eyes though baby blue at birth, were now dark, darker than space itself. Whereas a Black Hole entraps light and time, in a never-ending darkness. Void of all that he was, in the mirror image of his dark eyes he fought the memories. The reality that he could still not believe, let alone accept, they were gone -- stolen. In the mirror, he saw the depth coming. He would be forced to remember when he was complete, able to function in society, a time of peace, tranquility and balance. Oh the joy that filled his soul when she was born. A miracle of heaven and earth joined. He remembered a joy that nothing in the universe could replace. She was part of him, more than he would know. In the same "baby blue" eyes as his, he recognized she held an essence,

-- HER FATHERS.

The air became heavy, his legs shaking, failing now. It would soon be upon him, he must fight it or he would be lost forever. Remembering now the joy and trying to hold on to that which kept him sane. She was so precious, so fragile. As he held her in his arms, his life was complete now. Since he was sixteen years old, he knew he would have her, one child, a daughter. He knew even the name before she was ever conceived. Now, ironically sixteen years later, she was here, in his arms and a part of him. The family he had dreamed and longed for was here, he was complete. His eyes grew heavy with tears of joy, so tremendous that not even the waters of the great Niagara could compare to this wonder that he held in his arms.

Then without warning, they were gone. The loss now claiming his soul once again, in the mirror he desperately tried to hold on to her. However, the image in the mirror revealed what he now feared, He was losing ground to it, and it was

4

here. Slipping in to the "Escape", it was happening again. The loss as great as if humanity and his very existence; would be lost forever. The cold sweats had subsided, only to be replaced with the taste of bitter salt now flowing from his dark and void eyes.

A dark, deep loss, like the void. The "Escape", it was close now and he knows he must fight it. His grip on the sides of the sink tightened, until his skin was almost albino in color, from the loss of circulation. Once again, the mirror revealed the truth, the hurt, and the lies.

-- THE BETRAYAL!

Chapter Two

"Roots of Good and Evil"

Before Blake was even a thought his father knew as a young man, that working hard carrying 100lb blocks of ice up what seemed endless fights of stairs, to waiting families whose sustenance thrived only by his deliveries. He knew deep down within the cold blistering ice he carried delivery after agonizing delivery, that if he failed their precious sustenance for life itself would spoil and rot away. Depriving their family of the nourishment, they depended on for survival. Thus was born his father's deep devotion and drive. To do whatever it took to fulfill what he had set in motion, no matter the obstacles.

For it is said, "A man is only as good as his word". Moreover, his fathers words were strong as were his values.

Herein lay the source of Blake's values, forged in the hearth of his father.

Instilled and driven by the will to survive in a cold harsh world. The coalmines were no different, dark, cold and alone. His father knew someday he would leave this place, for a far better life where he could raise a family. This drive to make a better future knew no end. Nothing would stand in its way. Therefore, the journey began with his father and mother, the trek north to the unknown. A dream, a sparkle in two lovers eyes who wanted more. Who wanted better.

-- Who had to "***Escape***"

The beginning of their new life was born, a difficult delivery indeed. Where the bowels of the steel mills billowed a long grueling song of depth and despair. However, his father knew at the end of each day, his hard laborious work and drive to succeed, would yield him the time he longed for with his family. Day after Day, his father toiled without the smallest complaint. Fixed, focused on the hope this new future would bring him and his family, a new life. However, the rewards came neither quickly nor easily. They had to share even the smallest morsel of food. For it was all that they had. Yet neither gave way, for his father was "The Rock," honed from birth by granite values that could not be broken. Chiseled by his father's own strong hands. This is where Blake found his strength, his honesty and his values. Passed down thru his bloodline from father to son, these traits came neither cheap nor easily. Fused into the fabric of his essence. From generations handed down through years of experience, dedication

8

and the bond that held family together. Trials and tribulations were not unknown to his father, as the future would soon reveal. They could not have imagined what lie ahead on the path that they had chosen.

Chapter Three

"The Fire of Fate"

No! Awakened by the firefighter's alert pager Blake had thought for sure he had succumbed to the place of "Escape" forever. Sitting up now in his own bed, the pagers wailing alert telling him, peoples' lives were in danger. It had been a dream, no a nightmare of all nightmares. What if the pager had not sounded, pulling him back through the door of the "Escape," would he have been trapped in his sleep forever? His heart still pounding, sheets soaked with his desire to purge these memories from his soul. Doomed forever in that dark void, oblivious to anything outside of his new world.

This was no time to contemplate his fate now. The lives of people now depending on him were in his hands. Changing into his fire/ rescue clothes kept always ready, near his bed, he grabbed the pager to listen to the emergency broadcast call to all volunteer firefighters at Station 5. He dressed quickly as time was literally a matter of life and death. As the pager sounded a series of tones, alerting fire/ rescue volunteers, it seemed as though it was two fold. To help save lives as well as his own by pulling him back through the door of the "Escape" before it had a chance to close on him forever.

Now dressed and racing to the station where the tools to save lives were stored, the pager sounded again preparing for the information to follow. "Structure Fire!" came first. He had fought many a structure fire in his time. As he drove he wondered why he had volunteered for fire/ rescue, but deep down he knew why. The pager cracked again "Structure Fire!" his heart jumped! Time was now critical the structure would not last long. He could see the glow as he drove the engine closer to the site at where his training and courage would be tested. He knew the reason. -- Felt it deep inside.

He needed the rush that only came from deep within the

throat of a fire. To tempt fate with his very own life as to say,

"Fate will not conquer here this time". Like a knight in shining

armor, he must risk all to vanquish the evil he knew so well.

The heat was high now, the throat of the fire just ahead. The

radio brought him suddenly back to reality. Child reported in

back bedroom!" Blake's heart seemed to stop. Staring now

at the throat of the fire, the face of evil would have to wait

this time. A precious life hung in the balance. A life not yet at

it's full potential. He abandoned his fight with fate. He knew

well the pain of loss. He could not bear for another father to

feel the loss of his daughter as he had. Making his way to

the back of the structure, there in the corner, huddled in fetal

position, was a precious child, brought to life by the passions

of her parents. He called out to her, as she lifted her head

she responded, "DADDY? Daddy where are you?" Blake's

stomach sank, for he knew in his heart his own precious daughter had uttered those very same words years before when he had spoken to her on the phone after they had left. She was young and could not understand why her father was not there with her. The child stretched out her arms to a figure barely seen in the dense smoke. Fate would not claim this child, not here, not now. He embraced the child with the same urgency and care as if the child's own father had been there in his place. Outside he carried the precious life to her mother who waited with uncontrollable horror! "MOMMY!" she yelled with out stretched arms.

The drive home was exhausting. Diverted from tempting fate with his own life, another had been saved. Still he felt he had been cheated. The longing for the void to be filled. The fire he fought had neither claimed him nor released him. Now at home, the smell of the fiery remains, were strong on his flesh. A refreshing shower was all that was needed to remove what once had been a family's home.

The "Escape" would not find him now. He now laid awake

hearing and seeing the precious child in her mother's arms.

Fate would not prevail. Time and circumstances had been

altered. He had challenged fate and won, this time. He lay

now in wonder. Why had they taken what had been his? His

body and mind now exhausted, he fought sleep. For he knew

what it would bring. Yet a sense of calmness came over him

as the image in his mind of reuniting a family brought a spark

of hope to life. Drained of all emotion, sleep now had found

him, he would dream. Dream of he and his daughter together

again. In and out of consciousness, in the distance it was

soft, calling, and as close as if he could touch her. "Daddy,

Daddy -- where are you?"

Chapter Four

"Mother of Pearl"

A foundation is only as strong as the ground supported beneath it. This was his mother. For without her his father's fire to succeed would have been snuffed out, as cold as the steel ingots that he had forged lying cold and dark in the white snow. She was to say the least "A diamond in the rough." Pure, untouched and to his father more precious than the rarest stone ever found. In her eyes, he knew from the very first time he had seen her, that she was his one and only. His family, his bloodline would continue on, representing all that they stood for.

Through the worst and best of times she remained. The vows that bound them together in the beginning would carry them through until the end. These vows are sacred and not to be taken lightly. This he learned from the stories

15

his parents shared with him. As the years went by, the home movies they would watch together showed the love and commitment of the family. The family unit was sacred, the home a sanctuary protected from outsiders who would threaten their existence. Now with a new life growing, their own lives together were about to change. A first-born male would start the family unit that his mother and father had dreamed of long ago. This as every young wife needed and longed for. Helped to occupy the time while her beloved mate was toiling to ensure the future of their new lives together. Her time alone seemed endless, lonely, and almost non-existent. Each and every day she would kiss her mate goodbye, and then wait patiently as the hours slowly passed. Nevertheless, she was dedicated to their cause. She paid special attention to details. Everything must be right, and in its own place. For she had to keep busy to pass the time, These traits she practiced religiously, for when she would sit she began to think and feel the life that grew inside her. Soon the child would be here, to help thru the lonely days until her husband would arrive to complete the day and night. Together as a family, raised in the old ways. His mother was a good mother, both caring and thoughtful of all around her. Now living in a house of their own, this family unit had completed its first hurdle in life, --**SURVIVAL!**

Now with a child at home, her days were filled with new responsibilities. Each and every new task carefully inserted into her daily routine. All days were balanced as evenly as a highly skilled tightrope performer. For her day was now filled with endless care and emotion, which had to be carefully and skillfully given to Child, husband, family and home. This was who she had become. The order that held their new universe together. Her purpose in life now was clear. She was content. These new feelings partnered with new sensations and experiences were what she had longed for. For even with all this she still found time for herself. It was within herself that she found the drive and compassion to fulfill the needs of this growing family.

His mother was quiet, reserved and never missed anything. The household ran as a finely made Swiss watch with every detail personally crafted by her own hands. She was always there, always ready, Food and laundry, wife and mother, strong but loving. In her mate's eyes, she could have done no wrong. Never once had he heard her complain, nor did he ever hear his parents argue or fight. For if they did as all couples do, they did it behind closed doors and away from the children. For if there ever was a Mother of Pearls, one so perfect in every way, in his eyes, in his heart -- it was her.

<u>Chapter Five</u>

"A pearl of great prize"

He dreamt now so peaceful, His dreams always so real, so vivid. He felt as if he were there, not re-living them, but there as though the past had never happened. He longed for this to be true, before they were -- stolen from him, before the Betrayal, before the -- <u>*"ESCAPE"*</u>. Now in his dreamscape, the time is near. The life he has waited for, that he has helped to create, is minutes away. For years they tried his wife and he. Only to be denied the sweet comfort of a child by there joining. Nearly five days of labor she endured, as his child would arrive earlier than expected. As doctors painstakingly tried to stop the labor, to give this tiny precious life the time she so desperately needed for her lungs to develop. Each day the little one would try again, trying so hard for that miracle of birth. Yet more medication would be needed to help delay her awaited arrival. Blake stayed by their side sleeping on the floor not inches away if needed.

Then it happened! This time when she had tried to emerge, the little one was sideways. With no other option available, an emergency "C" section would now be preformed to save both the mother and child. His heart beat as though it would explode from the very soul that held it. This would be his only child, Blake new this in his heart and soul. As the doctor now, with hands as steady as a beam of light. Prepared to rescue these precious souls from their fate. Fate, he knew it well, for he had beaten it, cheated it and avoided it time after time. However, here he was, now, not in control of it. All he could do now was watch through the camera as he taped the entrance of his precious little girl before his very own eyes. Complications arose, but were quickly subdued by the skillful training of their capable doctor. She was here! In all her beauty, she was finally here. A miracle indeed just as he had dreamed all these years. Now in the tiny room, he

held his daughter. So tiny, so small, although two months pre-

mature, her heart was as strong as her will to survive. Gazing

into his wife's eyes, he saw his mate, beloved, and the one

with whom he had created a miracle of both life and passion.

For it was this love and passion, that brought his dream into

reality.

Now as his daughter slept in his arms, he remem-

bered when they had met, New Years Eve. Almost a full year

after the disaster of the business he and his brother had

owned. He had been coerced into showing up for his broth-

ers New Years Eve party. Finally, the bond of family gave way

above his anger. The party filled with customers, friends and

family. Music, dancing and chatter had filled the air; every-

one was having a good time. Blake felt as if he should have

fought the urge of family ties and wished he had the will to not

attend. Though the drive was a mere two hours, it seemed as

an eternity. He knew the reception would not go easily. There was still resentment between these brothers'. He remembered how it all began years ago.

They were eleven years apart. His parents trying for a girl, only to receive yet another son. The elder likened to their mother and Blake definitely to his father. For they were the same. Father and son. They would walk, talk, look and act alike. It was known to all that Blake should have been the junior, for he was the spitting image of his father in all aspects of life. Blake knew not of his brother as they were raised so far apart in years. By the time he reached the age of accountability to realize he had a brother, he was gone. Enlisting into the United States Air force. Blake knew only of his brother through home movies, pictures and the stories his parents shared with him. He idolized his missing brother.

As to a child lost and waiting to find his missing sibling. Now years later after graduation his brother phoned and asked him to move to that Lone Star state and try to recapture the time they had lost. Many good times were had, as Blake found his missing brother. For they were family, of the same bloodline that had been separated but now were reunited with each other. Now driving in relentless rain, anger found him once again. He can still see and feel that day in the back room of the garage, fists drawn in rage and anger between brothers. The accusations brought forth again time after time. Blake had covered for his blood brother, even evaded his brother's wife about his whereabouts and many affairs. For he was his brother, the same blood ran through their veins. "Blood is thicker than water" this is what his father taught them. Always put the family first. Be true to your bloodline. Protect it and never betray it. However, it had gone too far. No more lies. Blake could not take it anymore. With lowered fists, he echoed, "It's not worth this anymore" and ended the relationship he had sought for so long.

Now wiping single tears from his eyes, he regained his composure and opened the door. He was greeted first by his brothers' wife. She was always happy to see him and while hugging him whispered, "I am so glad you decided to make it". He forced a false smile as best he could, still holding onto the lies and the truth. He could not, dare not, break his bond to family. It was not his place. They were still brothers, bound by family and blood. Blake could feel him watching, wondering what he would do and say. Nevertheless, Blake held his bond and silence and quieted his tongue. It was not the same; they talked, drank and even laughed at the past. However, something had changed, they both knew that. It was time to go; this effort was meaningless. He made his way to the office to use the phone to find a place to stay the night. As he opened the door, he met her. There she was his wife to be. However, he did not know it, nor did he know who she truly was. Startled by his entrance she replaced the phone on the hook. "So you are the brother we have been waiting on?" She asked. His reply was a disinterested, cold and bleak as the weather outside had turned. For his only goal was to leave this place. "Yes so what?" Blake replied. It seemed strange as he heard it echo. Not at all, like him. He was always polite to others, especially those he did not know. He apologized and stated that he just had to get out of here. She smiled as if to say, "Stay awhile" and they began to talk. She was comforting, her eyes held a special beauty, deep and mysterious. He had been "caught up" in her conversation as they laughed and danced. He had seen her, recognized her. Maybe a past customer. Yet he could not recollect. Regardless, he was smiling again, happy and dancing away. He would see her again. -- Soon!

<u>Chapter Six</u>

"The Origins"

Blake grew up in the long since named "The Dirty City". In a loving family, in a nice neighborhood on the edge of town. The family had grown now though not by any means on purpose. Two beautiful baby sisters had joined the family a decade later. Again, one likened to their mother, the youngest. In addition, the other to their father. A family of four, two boys and two girls. His parents though unprepared were happier than ever. They had been blessed two fold again. Ironically, Blake's differences from his brother to his sisters' ages were similar. Coincidence would be the only explanation anyone could ever find out, or was it? As he grew up no more than a decade later, he himself would leave the fold as his sisters' reached the age of accountability.

In school, he did well, straight "A" student in his younger years. His parents, so proud when offered the chance to attend an enrichment school. His parents agreed as to feed his constant hunger for knowledge. From the time he was young he was unstoppable. Constantly going, running out the doors when ever open. Away from the house, out of the yard. His parents seeing their sons need for exploration had to fence the entire area just to keep him in. Here lie his ambition and desire to experience all he could. His father a natural born "Jack of all trades" had a limitless supply to offer his young son. Music, sports and auto repair were some of the most interesting experiences he would ever learn. He like his father had inherited this art of "Jack of all trades". His first love was of music. His father who played solely by ear had mastered the piano and encouraged him to play. Side by side they would play, father and son. The latter picking out notes as his father played a toe-tapping tune.

Gifted with his fathers' ear for music, the notes and tones came surprisingly easy to him. He could hear and feel the music playing on his 45 rpm player he kept by the piano. His first song he would master, "Floyd Cramer's Last Date". With each note played over and again, picking up the needle and starting again until he got it perfect. Oh! the joy and fulfillment that playing this music with his own hands brought. It would be with him the rest of his life. His solace in times of need. He took quickly to all things his father taught him. The same dedication and quest for knowledge knew no bounds. The world was there, waiting for him to discover all it had to offer. His father taught him mechanics in their small backyard garage. Father taught son, and son taught father. However, both were the same. Both had little patience, yet a bond between them as a teacher to a student, instilling all his knowledge to pass on to his son. This is where the strong bond between them was formed. His father associated mechanics to life itself, so that a young child might easily understand. The car to the human body, the wheels to his legs, the body of the car to his body, the engine to his different body parts. This is where he learned to simplify and associate things in life. To effectively communicate. Simplicity, in its simplest form, for this is where his father had taught all he would know in this small garage. Their place together shared by father and son. Where bonds were born, secrets told and memories, stories and lessons learned. This is where it all began, who he would grow up to be. Like his father had become, was what Blake wished for. To be exactly like him. For he honored his father and lived for the day that he could make him proud of his son. A family of his own like he grew up in, house to remodel with his children. Moreover, a child to pass his heritage on and raise in his families ways combined with his own. A job to work hard at and retire from and a loving and supporting wife like his fathers to grow old and settle down with. This is where he learned about life. Where his father taught him all that he needed. Where his common sense was instilled.

"You are the sum of your experiences" and Blake was experiencing more and more each day. School was an untouched universe of new life and he would see it all. Sports and music, these he excelled in the highest. His drive to do his best and attention to detail drove him to succeed in school. Academically biology and anatomy held his interest. His father had paralleled the human body to automobiles. It was intriguing to apply this method of comparisons to his studies. Seeking unfailing understanding in learning how it worked in every detail. This drove him to try to understand it and learn how it worked. These and many more experiences would feed his hunger for the knowledge he craved. These times were the building blocks of his life, as he would soon find out. Then graduation came. Things would change -- Situations would be different now. Life itself would try to replace his fathers' garage

<u>Chapter Seven</u>

"Purity of Love"

Awake now, his sleeping pearl in his arms. His beloved peacefully at rest after the stresses placed upon her body and soul. Her personification of inner and outer beauty was as comforting as the pearl in his arms. He remembered their beginning five years ago. He had moved back to their hometown he had left to be with her now. He had always enjoyed doing little things to see the surprised look on her face when she discovered them. A taped rose to the window where she worked, acting out characters in the movies they watched together. He remembered the first of such a movie in her fathers' house, "Tarzan the legend of Greystoke". His childish mood now invoked. They had been lying on the floor watching when as the ape on TV wrestled with Tarzan, so did he with his Jane. As laughter filled the air, this was a special time.

They did all they could together, retreats with family to the lake, fishing and hunting. Family retreats and holidays. All were special and each one brought a special closeness between Blake and her family. What he had sought for so long he now believed was possible. He remembered that special evening, like no other, created to become deep-seated in her memory. He had taken off work early that day to prepare everything. The timing had to be exact, everything in its place. For this would be a tale she would be asked over and again to recite. It would never fade from her memory this he knew. The stage was set, candles and wine placed in front of the fireplace that ran from the video player to the televi-sion. Light low and soft music playing, the time was near. He met her at the door clad in only a towel. The look upon her face was priceless, worth keeping all things secret. He asked her to trust him, yet she was speechless with wonderment at what indescribable experience he had prepared for her.

For he was always doing out of the ordinary things to mystify and surprise her. Eyes closed was essential, the suspense must build. Seductively he removed piece by piece every bit of clothing she had placed upon her body earlier. As hands and lips caressed her skin that was revealed by each article removed, her breathing increased. Her heart now pounding as she now stood before him in all her essence of beauty. Anticipation of the unknown had now taken control of her.

Leading her now to a sitting position in front of the mock fireplace, he placed the chilled glass of wine in her hand and whispered to her, "*Open your eyes*". Blake knew from the look upon her face that this moment would be remembered. Both naked now, symbolizing the baring of their very souls to each other. The look on her face was that for which he had hoped. Amazement and wonderment came simultaneously. This was how he had proposed to his beloved. With ring in hand and literally baring all, her smile filled with laughter and of slight embarrassment, she accepted his proposal as he slipped the ring upon her finger.

As his eyes opened slowly, Blake noticed his beloved was not in her bed. His daughter now not in his arms. A quick glance to the crib. -- EMPTY! Maybe they had been taken for tests. In addition, they may have not wished to wake him. The hospital ward was oddly quiet, with no sign of a single member of staff. Something was wrong. He could feel it deep within his now chilled bones. Even the lighting seemed dim, almost as though he was in a cavern deep underground. The air itself had become damp, stale with a musty scent. Picking up the phone to find someone who would know what had happened to his precious family, he discovered the phone was -- dead! A chill ran thru his body now. He must find them! Now in the hallway searching, crying out to them. He heard nothing but his own voice echoing through the halls. Where was everyone? A fully staffed hospital could not just disappear! Every door he checked, the rooms were empty. Not a soul in sight! Just as he let go of the last door in the hallway it disappeared from his very sight! Startled he turned to see the entire hallway disappearing as he watched! Where were they? What was happening? Then he saw it. Devouring everything in its path! The *"VOID"* was after him now, again! As fast as he could run past the doors, the walls ahead of him were disappearing. It was closing in on him. He could feel its presence like a cold breath on the back of his neck. Faster! Faster! He had to make it to the elevator at the end of the hall. The building itself now dissipating. The roof gave way to the blackness, void of all stars. Almost there, only a few more feet. He slammed the elevator call button so hard that it sent vibrations thru his whole body. Then it just disappeared. He turned in fear.

-- The *"Escape"* was almost upon him!

<u>Chapter Eight</u>

"Young at Heart"

Though his sisters, only thirteen months apart, were as precious to him as to his parents. Blake enjoyed helping his mother take care of his younger siblings. He had seen babies before but never so close and he so interested in them. So tiny in the loving arms of his father, his parents were so proud of these new additions to the family. He remembered, as they grew up closer together all the things he had made his younger sisters do. From scratching his back to tickling his feet to no end. He loved them so. Nevertheless, he to would leave the fold soon. Now, similar to his father, he also employed by the same company to work. He wanted so to "follow in his father's footsteps". He worked hard and learned all he could. Several times working double shifts to help build for his future family. After pulling double shifts all week, he was physically and mentally drained. He welcomed his promotion to inspector. That was where he had met his first, although through school he had experienced many things, he had recalled the vividness of his father's rendition of the so-called "Birds & Bee's." this kept him abstained from the actual act, though mostly from fear itself.

Even so, he had met her there, a stunning blonde-haired woman. He could not keep his eyes off her. Then it happened, he had been caught! However, he did not look away, their eyes met and they new -- for they would have to meet. When shift ended, he wondered if they would ever meet. Yet there she was, standing at the gate waiting on him. They agreed to meet at the local pub where a handful of workers always went. There they talked and laughed about work. Although, ten years older than himself she would teach him all he would ever need to know. More than he could ever imagine. He awoke that morning a full-fledged man. A different outlook on life was now in his eyes. However, the fears

from his father's words were not forgotten! They were now

to be buried, deep by what he had learned and experienced.

The additional teachings his father gave him of women, were

also fortified by this night of overwhelming ecstasy. "Always

take care and put the woman first" was his only rule his father

had given him about women. The rest will take care of itself.

He was right in things of women, and Blake learned just that.

What is given first in all things will be returned seven fold.

Blake learned many things from his father, though

simple at first he always learned later the sophistication of

how and why his father had taught him. First to see and

understand the simple side, which in turn would reveal the

complexities, with an open mind His journey into the real

world had begun. The future was in his hands and he was

eager to explore and experience it. Now with the new knowl-

edge and feelings of his first real relationship, it seemed all so simple. Now, as he lay drifting off to sleep, content and happy

that he would dream of all he had just learned on this new

road he would need to travel.

<u>Chapter Nine</u>

"The Awakening"

Jesus! The sound of the alarm clock had wrenched him from his nightmare. Again, he had almost succumbed to the "Escape". Now drenched as before, he stood in front of the bathroom mirror. Deep in his eyes now, he stared, deep into his very soul. When would this stop. So close this time. Again he wondered what would have happened if the alarm clock had not sounded at that precise time. This time as always, his nightmare was as vivid as ever. However, he remembered dreaming within this nightmare that same dream too, it was as real as the nightmares, yet they were filled with joyful, happy times. He wondered how thin these lines were between reality and insanity. He now remembered when his oldest friend the artifact diver, had found him lying there in the same place that he now stood. It had been three days since

41

anyone had heard from him. His answering machine and cell phone now full of messages. However, his trusted employees kept his business running and they to began wonder about the lack of contact and direction from him. Here deep in the "Escape", in the fetal position, He lay, shaking, weeping and unaware of his surroundings. The loss too heavy to bear, he had retreated, no! Given in to the void of the "Escape". Here now where all was lost he felt nothing. He became nothing. Though the lack of feeling and being, gave neither pleasure nor pain, it had shielded him, removed all sensations and memories. This was the price to pay, to relinquish his very soul to where his loss would not exist, when the betrayal had never happened, here in this place, he would never dream. Neither asleep nor awake, deeper into the "Escape". Here he could never be hurt or loved, praised or belittled, rich or poor, triumphant or defeated. Here nothing could be given and most of all, here nothing could be taken away. In the

"Escape", he ceased to exist. Now being pulled back from this "Escape", his oldest friend could not have known what he had done, rescued or condemned. Neither knew what the out come would bring. Now trusting his oldest friend to silence, he shared what had happened. He understood never to voice what he had just witnessed or what he would soon hear. Blake trusted no one but his oldest friend, as for now he became his only family. He had never failed and was always there. Requiring only their friendship and expecting nothing in return. When Blake had first moved to the sunshine state he had been his first friend. At a surf shop, he had beaten him down on price on a simple wetsuit already on sale. They talked about it often through the years, which always ended in hysterical laughter. Thus this friendship had been born. Now it would be tested, for all time. For what he had seen, and would soon be told, might even change his outlook on Blake himself. Even on the world, as he knew it. The next few hours seemed endless as the story unfolded. With each word he spoke, the pain and anguish took its toll, and was revealed in his face and eyes. For ten years, he had been married. He had finally attained what he had longed for, and searched for. A family of and like his own. A loving wife and beautiful daughter. A prospering business in the oldest city in America, A home nestled outside the city. A place to raise there child and grow old together. The seasons here were unmatched, with spring, summer and fall so beautiful it had rivaled many vacation spots around the globe. Though winter and the snow it brings, would never find this place, yet the snowball that would crush him, began to ascend as an avalanche toward an unknowing sleeping city. Now in his living room, to a single trusted friend, he would bare his soul and reveal what he had discovered. They were gone. He had been, *betrayed!* He now saw The Intent. He now felt,

-- The Ultimate, Betrayal.

Chapter Ten

"A Cousins' Bond"

The reality of life itself began, as swiftly as his journey had begun. The age difference was too great, now the loss of his first relationship with the stunning blonde-haired woman marked a stepping-stone in his young new life. What path to follow now, he asked. Only his own voice echoed in his mind. A simple phone call to his cousin in God's Country would be needed now. Young, hurt and money in hand, he had turned to youthful wants and needs. He and his cousin were close, and now after his first relationship had failed miserably; it was time to broaden his horizons. He would experience his first rebound.

He had phoned his cousin and informed him of what had happened. Though each was a little wild on their own, together they would make an asylum look sane! He learned from his cousin that life was to be experienced, and so it would be. Always when he had driven down, they would have remarkable experiences! Once his cousin had pushed him to the edge in his dodge ram truck, four wheeling straight up and then down a hill so steep as to take his breath-away.

He knew he would have to repay this experience though, and shortly after in his cousins hopped up Camero, Blake drove as both his cousins joined in derogatory words and phrases as he down shifted and slammed the pedal to the floor! Squeezing the Camero between the car on their left, and the side of the bridge to there right. Whoosh! With an equal level of pure fear, echoing thru the car. Justice had been served! *Cold.*

He had asked his cousin to set up a double date to help take his mind off the pain of his recent heartache. More-over, as always his cousin complied. The young women were smiling and dancing and with a wink of gratitude, he showed his gratefulness to his cousin with a simple yet understood gesture, the squinting of eyes with the smallest nod. Blake continued to see his newfound love, though he would have no idea she would become his first betrothed. Taken in by her beauty, and youth as well. Though younger than Blake, He out of Fear that an older woman would repeat what had happened previously. He remembered his talk with his father in the garage. "Marry one young and raise her with you as I did". Now seeing his father and mother so complete and happy together he once again "followed in his fathers foot-steps", though warned by his cousin he would neither heed, nor listen to his cousins' word of warning.

A minister related to her family married them in her mother's house due to His own parent's disapproval of the marriage, as well as his fathers' refusal to give his blessing. They felt he was too young and not ready for marriage less than three months since he had met her. His life was renewed again. They shared many new things together as he would teach her with love and passion, what had been taught to him in the heat of a single night. Life was good again, His heart mended by their love and touch of another. No man could want for more.

Work that particular day would not be the same as it had been. He was now being promoted as the youngest assistant Forman the factory had known. Pride rose inside of him knowing his father and bride would be proud of him. Now given the rest of the day off, he would stop by where she worked to give the news in person. Now on the way home he wondered why she had not been at work. Walking from his car he noticed his wife leaving the complex, but not in her usual uniform. His heart sunk, as if a thousand torpedoes had just penetrated a submarine bound for its homeport. As he followed her, he had hoped he was wrong. However, his heart would take yet another tear, after confirmation of his worst fear. He returned home and packed all her things. Now on the road back to God's country he drove to meet her mother. He had phoned his mother-in-law on the way back to the apartment and had arranged for her to meet him halfway and explain why. He had no choice. She had betrayed their love and trust. Being under the legal age, he would return her to her parents pending a divorce. Each mile he drove the silence felt like a giant weight upon his shoulders.

Now on the road she offered no excuse or reason. If she had, he would have turned the car around right at that moment. Now watching as his wife drove away with her mother, he was drained of all emotion. His heart now barricaded by a thick wall of hurt and pain. He would not know love again nor would it find him. For he was lost on this roadmap of life, with no one to guide him.

Chapter Eleven

"Last Hope"

In the mirror now, he saw what was left. A shattered soul in a shell of what he used to be. After a long hot shower, he had decided not to work today. He called his secretary to reschedule his appointments and not to worry. Now in front of the TV. He began again from the beginning. First, his wedding video, where he had sang, "My Only Love" to his bride to be. As tears now filled his eyes, he sang with the video softly, reminded of how deep and how much they had shared. As the older of his two younger sisters played the accompaniment, he watched and sang as though he himself were there. As the vows were being pledged, he, so caught up in this joyous time, recited them as well. "For better or for worse, in good and in bad times, in sickness and health". As the tears grew larger so was the tightness in his throat. As they, both spoke "Till death do us part." He felt at this very moment that death had come, for life, as he knew it had been intentionally taken from him, a living death he has now been forced to endure.

Now in front of the mirror once more, the "Escape" would claim him no more. The end of the police revolver that he had kept was cold and hard against his temple as the tile floor he was standing on. He could no longer endure the living death that tormented his days and nights. Confused with the loss of his family he looked deep into his own eyes, he saw the void itself. The "Escape" never came for him. It was deep inside him. Feeding on his misery. It had consumed him. Pulling him deeper and deeper to the edge of a total loss of control. He played every scenario out in his mind, but they all ended the same. They were still gone, Stolen and betrayed. In the mirror now, the blackness of his pupils seemed as though they had expanded, and now covered the iris of his eyes as if to say, "Escape" -- "Escape" is here, inside your-self." "Here, where no one or thing can hurt you". "Where the pain of loss can never be felt". Where nightmares cease to exist yet replaced with a sweet, silent bliss. Yet he knew if he let himself "Escape" again, he would never return to his world. It would claim his very soul. The hammer of the .357 revolver made a cold hard click, as it locked into place by his thumb. He could not, would not allow the "Escape" to consume what little he had left of his sanity. He would end his torment now by his own hand. No one could take that from him. His living death, would be ended, and yet be replaced by what waited for him on the other side. In the background, the reception video was finishing. His heart slowed to what seemed an almost lifeless beat. His loss now, feeling as heavy as if the weight of the earth itself sat upon his shoulders. The mirror revealed all he had lost, all he had become. Yet it could not reveal what was ahead on this path, he had now chosen.

His eyes locked now, on the image of himself, layer upon layer of dried tears covered over by a thin glistening sheen of hope. As he stared deep into the void of his own soul, he saw the "Escape" coming. This time it would not calm him. He would face it now, and forever end its need to enslave him. As the reception music ended, the time had come. Facing his inner soul the "Escape" was here. Waiting for him to choose. Face to face with his mirror image, he was prepared and ready for the task at hand. He looked into the void, squeezed the safety off, and then stopped! The sound now echoing from the TV/VCR was his daughter's voice, "Daddy"! Echoing through the house. The sound of laughter and the love of a child. So great, and so powerful. He lowered the revolver, and tears streamed down his face. He could not lose her again. He could not deprive her of a father. He would be there for her, love and cherish her. She would not forget or lose her father, she was his hope, and she was his strength.

She had brought him back from the edge of death itself. For within his love and devotion to his daughter he would find the strength and will to rebuild his life and heal.

Chapter Twelve

"A New Life"

Now with his first relationship and his first marriage in failure, he wondered what else could happen. Nevertheless, to all who have spoken those very words, know that fate will seek out and answer that very question. Now without any warning, retrieving his paycheck from the mail was included a pink layoff slip, with no known date for return. Again, he thought of how fate had answered his question, yet fate was not done, not yet. Now shuffling thru the mail as if a deck of cards, fate held the ace in the hole. Bills he had been unaware of, tremendous bills. The drastic change started with a call to his older brother in the Lone Star State. After a short conversation, he had been convinced to move there by the promises of his older brother. With no work to be found in the "Dirty City", he would head to the southwest in search of a new life and a reunion with the brother he had never known. The meeting was as he had anticipated. A long lost feeling now manifested face to face. The connection and bond between them was strong. Both were weeping as they embraced. Blake had dreamed about this reunion with his brother for as long as he could remember. The time to start a new life was at hand. Leaving his failed attempts in the Buckeye state, this would be a fresh start with new surroundings and a new-found family member to embrace. The days and nights that followed would prove many new feelings and experiences, with his brother. From fishing and hunting to lifting weights and spending time with his family. They did everything they could together, all the time. Both could not wait to see the other. His brothers' wife, a local nurse, nurtured their lost relationship, for without her understanding and patience, Blake's reunion with his brother would have been a severe intrusion in their family life. She had always treated him with respect, and allowed him to interact with the family as a whole. This made him feel at ease and earned a special respect for this local nurse in his family circle.

He would experience a completely new life style here. Cowboys in Parker Square, where he first learned to country western dance and had his first date since moving to the Lone Star State. Things were different here, but he soon learned to adapt and fit in. It seemed now only a short time had passed since the nation's economy followed him to the southwest. Here again he felt the harsh taste of life. Once again, as another layoff would attempt to stop his forward motion in life. Faced again with a jobless economy, he felt like a gambler in Las Vegas, Winning enough to survive, only to lose it faster than betting the farm on a single hand. It seemed the house would always win. Blake folded as a poker player holding the worst hand a dealer could deal. With no other options, he decided to join the military. Now enlisted in the U.S. Air force like his brother had done before, he would leave the fold of friends and family. He looked forward to the structure and order the military would give his life. Basic training found a place for him, as he excelled quickly as squadron commander and honor graduate top in his class. Finally, life held no surprises for a Police Officer. Ensuring that law and order of his and many lives were protected against those who would oppose such things. His quest of knowledge was insatiable yet the military offered many avenues to help him quench his thirst. Focused now on his studies, and the need to achieve, he made rank quickly and earned the respect of both his equals, and officers. All that was -- seemed well. Here in the military he learned and respected order and found himself opening up to people around him again. He had known several acquaintances. His female staff Sergeant while instructing in class, made eye contact several times. Could it be? Order, structure and devotion to duty? It seemed worth the risk once again. Though hesitant at first, she had yielded to the dinner and movie he had offered. The day had started with a light soothing rain across the military base that seems to set the mood to help open the door to his closed off emotion. Now in civilian clothes they both regarded each other on the same plane. However, a short-lived intense romance, they had parted on good terms due to her promotion and re-assignment. How ironic he thought to have found someone so compatible and then to be taken away by the very thing that had brought him and her together. Watching now as she boarded the aircraft their eyes met again as if to say hope for the future had been restored by what they both had shared. Watching the 747 fly against the blue cast sky, it resembled a white dove reminding him of the hope, which had been instilled in – and had mended a broken heart.

<u>Chapter Thirteen</u>

"Dedication of Love"

With each video that he watched now, he saw his daughter growing up in a new light. In the past, he would watch his precious little girl grow up only by the videos that he would take when she would visit. He would watch them all from start to finish with the dedication of a deep loving father. By the end, he would be drained of all emotion and face soaked with tears. Now as he watched he smiled through those tears and rejoiced at what he saw in front of him. She would help him rebuild his life.

He would now turn to his first love. Sitting at the piano, he played and sang for hours. Sometimes into the early morning. He felt solace and comfort. He wrote a song for his daughter and taught her to sing it. "Daddy's Song." For it was special, and reinforced his love for her and told her that he would always be there to take care of her. They would sing it when they were together and when they talked on the phone. To hear her sing touched his very soul and kept him focused on rebuilding his life. She had inherited his talent for music and song as he had from his father. The phone calls and videos now became his building blocks on which to rebuild his life. The music and song would soothe and keep his mind from dwelling on his past.

At work, he tripled his effort to keep busy and continued building his company for his daughter's future. As time passed with hard work and devotion to his daughter, his sense of purpose and well being began to emerge. Blake looked forward to every visit as his daughter came off the plane running into his arms yelling, "Daddy! Daddy!" at the top of her lungs. It was always a glorious time when she arrived. Filled with trips to Disney, Universal and many other adventures. She would always be, "Daddy's Little Girl." He knows that -- deep in his heart and soul. Until the age of five,

he would have to pick her up and fly back with her. The busi-

ness prospered as time went by and he used, "get a way's" to

help fill the gaps when she was not there. His favorite place

was the Bahamas.

Chapter Fourteen

"A Bankers Friend"

Now on his way to work, always stopping by the bank to make the previous night's deposit. Always using the drive thru, it was abnormally full this morning. He decided to go in today. Standing in line, he noticed her in the adjacent office. Blake had first met her on the boat dock at his orthodontist's house. He was a good close friend, and they fished and deep sea dived together in the Atlantic Ocean. Many times Blake would find a calming feeling either in the depths of the sea or miles away from civilization itself on the oceans water. He could never repay his friend nor would he realize how much he had helped him to cope by letting him experience these new adventures.

Now in the bank his orthodontist's sister-in-law sat behind her desk. Since meeting her on the boat dock, he had wanted to see her. Yet he was still hurt and afraid to venture out again. As he knocked on her door, she looked up in surprise. A short conversation gave way to lunch and into a new relationship. Within the first year his interaction with her family as well as with his daughter, brought a new hope and feeling of rebuilding the family he had lost. The nightmares had not returned, for his mind and life were now occupied by his new relationship and family ties they had made. He had hired her daughter-in-law at his business, which would free up more of his time; she was both intelligent and trustworthy. Though the lifestyle he now faced was different from his own, he would embrace the change and welcome its comfort. The acceptance from her family and children meant a great deal to him. It seemed finally he had found someone to share his feelings with again.

As he lay next to her, it had been along time since the nightmares had ceased. He had enjoyed holidays now with his daughter and her family. Lying next to her, he felt a contentment he had not felt since before his family had been stolen away. He slept now soundly with her by his side. He had no way of knowing what the morning would bring. The nightmares and the hurt had ceased for now. He had hoped that they were gone for good. He now, booking a cruise for them to his special get away, and would invite her when she awoke next to him. As he drifted off to sleep, the awakening in the morning would not be the one he planned. Nevertheless, one that she had planned for him.

<u>Chapter Fifteen</u>

"Twice Bitten"

Blake had met his second wife to be, which he nick-named "Nae" through a mutual friend. Writing letters and nervous phone calls kept them in touch while he was in basic training. It seemed his romance with his instructor had restored faith and given hope in now, a new relationship that he would share with his second wife. Though she was the same age as his first wife, he would try once more to fulfill his dream of a family like his own. Now a Police Officer in the U.S. Air force with his new bride, they began their new life together. His life structured now and secure with his employment for their future, Blake studied hard and made rank quickly. It seems that life itself had smiled upon him once more.

It was a brisk morning in the state that housed the windy city. The base took on an almost ominous glow that morning. This would be the day; he had waited for so long.

Studying hard he was now up for promotion once again.

After roll call during the morning briefing, he had received

his third stripe in rank, senior airman. Congratulations from

his company officer and the day off given to him following

his promotion. Eager to surprise his wife he sped home with

the excitement of a child waking up on Christmas morning.

Pulling into the rear of the staff housing, he recognized the

staff sergeant leaving his house. His heart skipped a beat

then felt as if it had stopped. The excitement now fading from

view as though it had never happened.

As he gathered himself together, he entered his

home as if nothing had happened. He had to be sure, with

no room for doubt. He knew the staff sergeant though not

personally. That night he went to bed early knowing his wife

knew he had seen the sergeant leave. Blake heard a single

voice quiet and muffled coming from the living room. Return-

ing to the bedroom he unplugged the phone from the wall,
lifted the receiver, then plugged the phone back into the wall,
so he would not alert his wife that he was on the phone. He
listened long enough to confirm his suspicions. Repeating the
same scenario as to not be detected. With a heavy heart, he
stood in the doorway and motioned for her to hang up the
phone. She offered only the excuse of being bored during the
long days alone. Yet the damage had been done! He would
divorce again, -- in failure.

At the bus station, the air was thick as he said
goodbye and sent her home to her father. Blake could feel
the wall around his heart tightening its grip. He would not let
another deep inside again. He now lost his drive and interest
in his career, and now discharged from the military, returning
to the lone star state, he joined now with his brother, a family
business was born, as they began their journey together.
Blake teaching his older brother what their father had taught

him. The business flourished and they became well known and respected in town for their work and dedication. There father would be proud. Blake could not have wanted more. Together with his brother in business it seemed all was well again.

Though he did not notice at first, it was not long until Blake realized his brother leaving the garage for extended periods. Though this posed no problem in the beginning, he soon found himself waiting on parts to repair vehicles until almost past closing. That next morning he brought his concerns to his brother. As the bell rang at the gas pumps, his brother saved by the bell so to speak, announced he had this particular customer. Back to work in the garage, Blake focused on the vehicle at hand. Within a few minutes, his brother appeared and stated he would be back and was going to take this particular customer to work, and bring the vehicle back to be repaired, and for him to do the work on the vehicle. Several hours had passed before he noticed his brothers return. After repairing the vehicle, he again left to return this particular customer's car.

Blake could only assume in his mind what he knew all too well. Tired of covering his brother's tracks from family and friends, he would have to confront him and deal with this brother to brother. The morning air was tense as he arrived at work. This would not be a good day; he felt this -- deep inside his bones. His worst fears became known, shortly after his first cup of coffee. His brother's wife walked thru the door and asked where his brother was. Remembering his father's teachings, "always be true to blood" he replied, "Out for parts I guess." Though his mouth spoke one thing, his eyes voiced another. The feelings inside him were thick and heavy with despair. For he could not, it was not his place. They were brothers, of the same bloodline. Turning to leave he sensed she knew the truth, and knew he had covered for his brother.

When his brother returned, he asked where he had been this morning. Knowing he would not reveal where he had been, Blake recited the morning's incident. As allegations between brothers flared, and Blake knew the end was near. Now in the back room, fists drawn, these brothers' would be torn apart. Blake knew in his heart, he would have to leave for he had no family to support and he could not continue working with his brother. As he placed his set of keys on the desk and walked out the door, he remembered why he had moved here. To reunite with his lost brother. Now he was again back where he started, -- alone.

__Chapter Sixteen__

"Account Closed"

Blake awoke to the smell of fresh coffee brewing. This had been their ritual for over two years now. It was a special time in the mornings, where in the Florida room they talked and would greet the morning, and each other, with eyes that seemed to penetrate and see each other's soul. Basking in the warm sunshine that glistened thru the windows. The warmth of the sun and hot coffee helped to prepare them both for their day ahead. Now on the back patio the sunlight sparkled thru the water fountain that they had built together, as it cascaded over the edge into the reservoir beneath, it radiated -- peacefulness.

As she joined him on the patio, he sensed by her quietness, there was something on her mind. Christmas was around the corner, and it seemed as if this past year had passed by faster than his heart was beating at this very moment. It had been around this time last year she had kicked him to the curb so to speak, because of his response to her implications about marriage, He knew he was not ready after what had happened only a short time ago. Now feelings of deja-vu rippled thru his memory like the waves thru the half-cup of coffee he held. As she sat across from him sipping coffee, he admired her beauty as the warm sun caressed her face. The soft gentle morning breeze fondled her natural blonde hair, which gave her an almost pristine appearance. His brief moment of reflection, --broken by the very words he had feared earlier.

As she again recounted their history together, the question of marriage had surfaced once again. Blake knew deep down he was still not ready for this depth of commit-ment. Now, his eyes and presence, gave way to his answer before he could even speak it. Again easily as turning a light switch on or off, he found himself by the curb once again.

As before, she offered up the same reasoning, if marriage

was not in our future there was no reason in continuing the

relationship. Again, Blake tried to express his long-term com-

mitment to her, but his words passed by her as quickly as

the wind thru her hair. He had tried to become what she had

wanted, to fulfill her needs in every way. Yet the only need

she wanted so much, needed deep within her, He could not

yet fulfill.

<u>Chapter Seventeen</u>

"Sunshine"

Once again on his own. Blake finally agreed to attend the trivia game that night. A close friend of his had mentioned that a new woman they had hired was going to be there and that he should meet her. However, only a short time after his break-up, it would be a comfort to be among friends. As the game continued, his mind now redirected by the trivia questions, he still noticed as a Spanish woman sat down across from his friend who had invited him. Though he was asked here to meet another, she would not arrive for unknown reasons. His friend apologized, but he was drawn to this woman of Spanish descent. Her skin tone was as soft and darkened, as if she spent many of her waking hours on a warm beach, basking her smooth skin in the suns rays. His friend introduced them and at that moment, it seemed as if all around them had ceased to exist. He knew he would see her again.

As they drove home along the beach highway on their first date, they felt comfortable, natural around each other. The evening had been going so well it seemed as though fate itself had brought them together. As they talked, with each glance he became aware of her natural beauty. How her lightly darkened skin was in balance with her blonde hair, her sensuous soft smile, as bright as that of the sun and captivating eyes. Thus, he called her "Sunshine" from that day on. He now remembered the cruise he had booked to the Bahamas. Would she go? Did he dare ask? Before another thought entered his mind, he had asked if she would like to go. Though only a single second had passed, it seemed an eternity. As quickly as he had asked she had responded, "Yes, I would." Both were stunned now by the question as much as her answer, they laughed and talked about their future voyage all the way home.

The ship sounded its last call to board. At the entrance to the main deck, they both paused for a ship's picture of their moment together, and signaling of the beginning of the voyage forward. As the ship departed port, they stood on the deck and watched as the Eastern seaboard faded from view. After dinner, they had both enjoyed the wine tasting the cruise had provided in the lounge. There were many experiences offered on the cruise, as in life itself. He sensed a sort of naive ness about her, almost as if she had lived her life in the shadows unaware or worse, not allowed to experience the joys and pleasures that life can bring. As the night came to rest on the oceans bed, so they lay together side by side. He had promised her no strings attached and he knew he would not violate his word. Even now as he lay beside her, his longing for her was pure, and deeply felt. Her feelings would prove to be the same. As the night was caressed by the soft waves against the side of the cruise ship, she turned with the same gentle touch. For her first time, her wants, her needs, had been put first, and together she would venture into unknown, uninhibited passions and pleasures.

Chapter Eighteen

"A New Year"

Now living in Dallas Fort Worth, Blake received a phone call from his brother who he had not talked to in almost a year. After several calls, he had agreed to come to his New Years Eve party. He had met her there. He was on the way out leaving the party when they crossed paths. "Cin", which he would nickname his third wife, had asked him to stay, and they enjoyed the party together. Their relationship continued and he was finding himself moving back to be closer to her. Employed by a national pizza chain he settled down in this small comfortable valley. He remembered how he had courted her with a zest and passion all its own. She came from a small farming town just across the Red River. It seemed as though they had everything in common. He had never met a woman so simple yet graced with her own beauty as well as a zest for life. His life seemed to revolve around hers. Several relationships had come and gone, but none compared to the passion he felt for her. He had fallen in love for the first time.

Living together nearly a year now, he embraced his newfound love. Her eight-year-old son was a blessing to both of them and Blake loved him as his own. He had longed to have a family like he grew up in and now it seemed all too near. Her family was special, he was certain of this. His interaction with their lives gave way to deep feelings of commitment and family bonding. Every holiday was spent in quality family surroundings, which touched his very soul. Her father a retired farmer had instilled within her his own zest for life. An avid hunter and angler, Blake enjoyed many a day in his company and grew to respect him as much as his own father. Her mother was also full of life, loved her family with an undying commitment of love. Always her family and spouse were first, in her life. A precious soul.

Her sister and brother in law were as close to Blake as his own siblings. He enjoyed and experienced all manor of family life with them. Their feeling of acceptance within their family circles instilled in him a comfort and stability he had so needed in his life. He remembered now when he had fallen in love with her. Her father's house on the floor watching "The Legend of Grey stoke" a Tarzan movie. Horsing and playing around he knew then she would steal his heart and be with him forever. He would ask for her hand in holy matrimony. This would be a special wedding. In their home church, which they attended, His sister would play the piano, family and friends from both sides would join them, in the bonding of two united as one. This wedding would be like none other, as his father would be present. Unlike the previous marriages, he did not attend or condone. He held his father above all in respect and honor, as his attendance and his blessing meant more to him than life itself.

Behind the white lace veil that separated them now in front of God and man, he sang to his lovely bride with all his heart. Tears that released the words and music from deep within his very being. Their sacred vows were to be next. Her eyes sparkled, were captivating with such love and compassion, as the minister repeated with solemnity the final vows, "Till death do you part." Her answer was as soft and delicate as the veil she spoke thru. Deep with in her eyes in her very soul he could feel the compassion as she committed her love and her life to him, "I do." How he loved her so, a part of him now was fulfilled. As he lifted the veil, her beauty had shown deep from within, a radiant glow that could only be matched by the aurora borealis that seemed to emanate from her now. As their lips met, their eyes closed, they became one. From deep within a kiss like none other he had ever felt. Facing family and friends their union together was now -- consummated. For the first time in his life, he felt complete.

Chapter Nineteen

"Bon Voyage"

As the ship pulled into dock, the last several days and nights had been unmatched by any experiences they had known. They had discovered a deep solace within each other's arms. Though both of them knew they had just rebounded from relationship, yet their desire to be in each other's company was strong, and manifested itself among their closest friends. The happiness they felt together could not be measured on any scale of this world. She wanted to experience all she could with him, all the things she had missed in life. Though she held a deep secret, in time, she would reveal it to him and he would accept and understand her arrangement.

From the moment they had met, "Sunshine" so properly named, shined as bright as the sun. A day or night did not pass by with out being in touch with each other. Her excitement with each new experience she shared with him, connected deeply, even the smallest of gestures and thoughtfulness were cherished and embraced by both. He found the little things he did meant so much to her, as well as bringing joy to him. Watching her warm and soft smile arise from these simplest of all mannerisms. Blake had fallen in love a second time though it had been many year since the first time he had felt those feelings. They talked of a new start together, down this happy path they had chosen. Her birthday was coming up and he had planned a special party with all their friends. A special present he had ordered to replace a treasure she had cherished so much but had lost. When she had opened the last of her gifts, he placed the box in front of her. As she looked at the box, her face was that of a child's Christmas morning, anxious yet unaware of what lie in the box in side. They all watched, as her eyes seemed almost dazed at the sight of a gold bracelet identical as to the one she lost and cherished so. Her look of astonishment gave way to a deeper look as her eyes rose to meet his own. He had touched a secrete place in her heart and forever would become part of her life.

The earliness of the alarm woke them both. He would be leaving soon for his fishing trip to the Bahamas. She, awake now, met him in the kitchen savoring the aroma of fresh ground coffee. As she walked thru the door, she was still wearing the white lace negligee he had given to her that night. The white lace against her dark tan skin and blonde hair captured her very essence as she walked thru the door. "Sunshine" was as bright as the heavens. Now they talked about their future together. As the words and ideas flowed from her soft lips, her excitement grew with each plan they put into place. When he returned, they would acquire a new condominium and furnishings as she hoped for a new start with no old memories. Learning that her daughter and children had no place to stay, he offered his home to them while he was away, so that she would not worry and would be able to find a new home for them to start their lives anew.

The warm tropical waters were both entrancing and soothing, as the first day of fishing had ended. Blake could not wait to get to the dock and call her back in the states. After several messages, he would try again after dinner. The native people here at the club were as friendly, as if they had known each and everyone here in the tournament as old friends. Blake excused himself to check the lines and reels on the boat for the next mornings run and try to phone her once again. By the third day without any contact from her, he called her sister who refused to tell him what was really happening. Now frustrated and far from home, he called once more, she answered.

The next several minutes would crush his heart and break his spirit, as a wild horse is by its tamer. She had been deceived and convinced to return to her previous relationship. Now on an emergency flight home he sat staring out the planes window, though what he saw was not what others would see in the field of beautiful clouds. How could this have happened? As the plane grew closer to home, he knew his fellow shipmates had understood and wished him the best on his return. Day after day, he would call until finally she agreed to meet. The tension in the air was as heavy as the weight of the world, upon Atlas's shoulders. As he placed all the pictures and articles of their relationship together on the table, her eyes filled with tears of regret and sorrow. Now both shedding tears of imminent loss, she could not bring herself to explain. As he placed the bag containing their memories in her hands, they embraced each other a final time. As she whispered between labored breaths of sorrow she replied, "I am so sorry." As he kissed her and closed the car door it took

everything, he was to say goodbye. As she drove away they

would both return to their previous relationships.

<u>Chapter Twenty</u>

"Birth of a Family"

The closeness between them was evident to all who met them. Both working in there community with family and friends close by. His younger sister, the elder of the two, had become very close with his new bride, who would one day bear his child, and helped to bring her into the family fold and make her feel at home. It seemed as if fate had taken a turn for the better in Blake's life, and now with family close by and nestled in this small community, the happiness and vision of his life would finally become a reality. They had talked many times about having a child. He, wanting to wait several years to ensure a stable marriage as well as being secure in his employment.

The pizza business had been doing very well for him in this small town. He wondered how life could be any better.

After several years, he was offered a promotion and bonus to manage in the oldest city in the nation. He had agreed with his wife every three to four months for her to return to visit her family, as their family were very close knit. The sunshine state was warm and welcoming. The Atlantic Ocean was an added pleasure as they had just moved into their brand new home on the Island. Their next-door neighbors to the north made them feel at home in the neighborhood, and became special friends as time went by. They had been trying now for several years to have a child. Yet try as they may they could not seem to conceive for almost four years now. Now as if darkness had found them, the promises made by his current employer were unfulfilled, as they were never intended to be from the beginning.

Blake had built a hobby in computers into a promising business that would now grow into far more than he expected. Though they continued trying to have a child, it seemed almost as if his dream of having a baby girl would now be denied. Each time his beloved had returned from the lone star state, he had noticed subtle changes within and about her. It was not long before she had issued the ultimatum to him. She would return to her family with or without him. This crushed his very soul! To choose between a successful business and return with no hope of employment, only to honor his beloveds wants and wishes. Blake was taught to honor the vows he had made. He would not forsake them now and would stand by and support his wife's wishes. The business now, would be sold.

Back in their small town, once again it seemed as though his wife was not as happy as he thought she would be. It was not long before he had found employment with a local coffee distributor, and the pressure of supporting his family would be relieved. It seemed as if a miracle had been granted to them. Though only a month had gone by, she had awakened him early in the middle of the night. Sleepy, and half-awake, a bewildered look now shown on her face, as she brought the news that she was with child. Oh the joy, that filled his heart and soul! So little, he had barely caught when she had questioned what they were going to do. Though he did not understand why she had replied this way, he was so overcome with a joy so deep within him. The remark had faded away as precedence for their unborn child filled his every thought.

The time was not yet near for his little girl to be born, yet she would not wait. Two months premature, this precious soul would not wait until her time. The doctors assured there were no problems ahead. They could not help but be concerned as for so long they had tried for her. His beloved now five days in labor, was shuttled to surgery where an emergency "C" section would have to be performed, as the child had turned sideways and demanded immediate care. He watched now as the doctor began. The sound of his child's heartbeat coming from the monitors seemed to be in perfect harmony with his own. Her feet were first; his excitement grew as her arrival to this earth began. No such wonderful a sight had he ever beheld as his dream unfolded now in front of him. This precious baby girl, conceived from the joining and passion of her mother and father, would be loved and cherished by their commitment to life. His dream now a reality, he had only to live his life out now, and enjoy his family. Yet what he would discover would shake the very foundation he had built.

Chapter Twenty-One

"Re-united"

As the boat docked, he met his captain and fellow shipmates returning from the fishing tournament he had been forced to depart prematurely. As he greeted them, he offered to help finish his responsibilities and unload and clean the boat. In their eyes, he felt their concern for him. He apologized for not being there for the team, yet they understood and welcomed his return. As he made his way to his captain's house, the banker had stopped by to visit with her sister. As they talked, it was imminent that they would be together again.

Even now, they became as close as if they had never been apart. Both confessing now in each other he revealed what had happened after they had parted last. Happy to be together again, there lives now moving forward in harmony

once again. They had reached a new level in their relationship. Moreover, they began planning their future together.
Thanksgiving brought a special place for them with family
together and the joy the holidays would bring. He felt comfortable around her family, for he had known them for many
years. Christmas was around the corner and he would surprise her in a most traditional way.

The dinner table had been carefully prepared with
his future sister-in-law's gift for décor. He had already made
aware his plans with the host and he agreed that this would
be a moment to remember. As family gathered and blessings
asked, all were present. The banker's father and mother, as
well as sister and brother. Timing would be critical for what he
had in store. For it would be chivalry in its purest form.

With the final remnant of this Christmas feast honor-
ing the birth of the holiest on high, Blake stood and raised
his glass in a toast to the family. Ring sized gift-wrapped

boxes were handed out to all the guests. A Chinese tradition he stated, each box contained a small scroll written upon each was a bestowment for the year to come. Happiness, contentment, health were among the few as each read them aloud. Last but not certainly least she would open hers last as planned. The look upon her face was priceless. As she opened his gift, she would receive a bestowment to out weigh all others. A two carat diamond engagement ring glistened as the light refracted from its surface into her eyes. Like a crystal chandelier greeting the morning sun.

Chivalry had not died out in this century as he stood before all. He passed the respect due her father for permission to ask her for her hand in marriage. Now that permission had been acknowledged, traditionally upon one knee, he placed his hand on hers. He could barely distinguish her heartbeat from his own, as both pulse rates seemed to beat feverishly in perfect harmony. Before she could answer he stated that her answer should be pondered upon and be rendered on New Years Day. His intent was two fold as to give her time to give serious thought, as to be certain, as well as to remove the pressure of her response with family encompassing her moment.

A new year, a new life together. Her answer had been a triumphant yes. The engagement had begun and all who knew him were aware the deep commitment he had taken based on his experiences. Life as well as his way of life would definitely change. He both embraced and welcomed this transformation of body and mind, soul and spirit. Each day seemed to bring newness as their lives were changing with every new thought they revealed to each other. Though she had accepted his proposal he could not seem to shake a feeling of concealment hidden deep within her. He had stopped by early this weekend morning to enjoy morning coffee with his fiancé. He had obtained a special gift he would surprise her with this wonderful morning, for the house. As the door opened his excitement now heightened, her kiss seemed with out substance and lack of passion.

Too excited and anxious, Blake placed the box he held upon the table. Coffee in hand his fiancé now in the Florida room sat quietly. As he began to open the box, she uttered a single sentence that would tear apart what little of his heart that had survived from the devastating loss of his family years earlier. He had finally been able to move forward again, yet as fast as his journey had begun, it would cease to exist with a greater velocity man could ever achieve. Tears now flowed from her eyes as she confessed she did not wish to be engaged. Though she would swear there was no other, Blake would later discover that her want and desire to attain the status her sister had achieved, had allowed herself to be deceived by another. A professor of manipulation had totally isolated her from her family, friends and life itself. A self-proclaimed author of Children's books would be the first of mis-representations the family would soon discover were without substance. Island house and status quo and many others, would be all revealed in his true character. Though aware of all this, Blake held himself and his life accountable for the complete failure of every relationship he had ever been involved in. deep inside his hurt and pain now transformed itself into contempt. He would never allow another so close to his soul again.

<u>Chapter Twenty-Two</u>

"Follow the Sun"

The economy in slump now, and with a new addition to the family, he found himself with out employment once again. There was no recourse but to return to the sunshine state and take a partner to rebuild his computer business. His responsibility now included a new life and he would not fail them. The packing had been tenuous as boxes were beginning to accumulate at a rapid pace. Packing the master bathroom, he discovered an unimaginable revelation. The small circular case was all too familiar. The dates stamped upon the pharmacy label had corresponded to the years previous when they had been trying to conceive. He remembered now what she had spoken that early morning barely a single month, since they had returned to the lone star state. A question he dismissed. Now in hindsight he was puzzled why she had asked what they would do about the pregnancy. However, he still did not understand why, it was only important that his baby girl was here, and he would focus on their future.

His business had prospered in leaps and bounds; working with a customer, they began erecting a new two story commercial building. His customer on the first floor and his business on the second. Much of his spare time as well as late nights, were spent in construction of the new facility. His wife had constantly returned to visit her family every three months, though financially they were far above any level they had attained in the past, she continually showed her lack of support and discomfort for returning to the oldest city. This evening he finished early, to head home to spend some quality time with his family. During dinner, she was specifically inquisitive about the business. She offered to help with the accounting, as it would keep cost down from hiring a secretary. She had never taken any interest before, and

Blake wondered what had brought about the sudden change of heart.

The caller I.D. showed a number from the buckeye state. As Blake answered the phone, he recognized the voice that echoed from the earpiece. He had not heard from his brother since his brother had abandoned the entire family after persuading their father and mother to retire in the lone star state. His brother, shortly after the family gathering, had left to return to the buckeye state, leaving all the family and his own children behind. Never had he called with any other intent than wanting or needing something. He seemed startled that Blake had answered the phone. As they talked, Blake inquired why he had phoned after all this time and what he needed. His reply seemed rehearsed as if performed by an actor, "can I not just call my own brother, just to say hello"? As they talked his brother asked how the building was coming along. Blake wondered how he knew, but dismissed it, as he could have learned when talking to their parents. He was relocating back to the lone star state to be close to his children.

His next statement would be both out of context, as well as out of character for him. He would be stopping by to see him, en route to the lone star state. Blake both wondered and asked why he would drive almost a thousand miles out of his way just to see him. Again, the same previous answer was rendered. He had no idea what his brother wanted, and told him to do what ever he wanted to do. The construction was going well and he would soon be able to relocate his business at the new location. Arriving home, he looked forward to seeing his family. Exhausted by his long hours, he always found time and energy as his baby girl met him at the door. Seeing his daughter was as if he was looking into a mirror, which turned back time itself. So precious and full of life she was the apple of his eye, she literally held his heart and soul within her nature.

Now asleep his little girl at rest, his wife now presented him with what would be the single most devastating event he thought he could ever experience. The divorce papers were clear and simple. She wanted to move back home with her family and take his baby girl with her. As the days and weeks passed, she had convinced him that he had been the problem. Ranging from removing her from her family and friends and having to remain home with her only career, raising their child. The hurt and pain he felt stimulated every nerve in his body, to the highest threshold a human body could tolerate. He struggled to hold this family together yet she would not give in. His will now emotionally broken, he would now concede. Yet he would discover a far more earth shattering betrayal.

Chapter Twenty-Three

"A Dream Attained"

Driven now by the humiliation of opening that part of himself, which he had guarded for so long since the loss of his family. Blake found himself once again in a state of despair and loneliness. It seemed as if he was destined not to have a companion or even a relationship. For every one he had been close and opened his heart to, had shattered it into more pieces than stars in the known universe. He felt no heart at all left within him. He had no love to give, He had no life to look forward to.

Now drained of emotion, Blake turned his sights and interests to an Oldies local club. His dance skills and personality had won him favor and status with the owners and patrons in a very short time. Now in his element he would run wild and free, with no one to tie him down. Soon he became part of the club by working in the DJ booth and creating, as well as performing skits for show on the dance room floor. It seemed he had finally found his nitch. Now the dreams and nightmares had not found him this time. As he sunk deeper into the roll of Mr. Lucky, that he had been nicknamed by the club owner. Lucky, this as he looks back, would never have been a name for him. Yet in this club, he was just that. The following year was tremendous with all that he could hope for as a single man. It seemed as though he was destined to be single. As mid life came in full swing upon him, he had no crisis, and embraced what it had brought to him.

As the internet unveiled itself to the world, Blake could see what would become of his computer business, and placed it on the market for sale before the web could dominate the market. With his business sold, he went to work in sales with an old friend, The Brit. Now free from an office he would continue a new start, of a single life on the road and free. He focused now even more on his first love --music. A co-worker,

he had started off with on the wrong foot with years before,

now became his roommate. Fellow musician and adopted

brother to replace the one he had lost. Music had healed now

what had hurt him so much. When his daughter visited, she

would join in and sing, as she had been gifted with the same

talent he and his father shared. Connecting with his daughter

in this way gave him a peace in his soul none could imagine.

Blake met a customer and friend, who would invite

him to play and join in a local band that was growing and

needed a keyboard and sax player. Soon his talents helped

the band to move forward and venture out into the internet and

beyond. Joy had filled his heart now, being part of this mag-

nificent band. Now a dream of his own had been fulfilled, on

the stages in the sunshine state. His daughter now beaming

with pride, as she watched her father perform. Blake would

hope and pray that she would continue with her own musical

talents and one day join her father, that they might perform on stage together. It seemed all had worked out for the best and Blake now with a full schedule every week, had little time to sit and ponder on his past. Life was vibrant and waiting to be lived and he would do just that, live it to its fullest.

Now fully involved with the band and the club, he hardly had time to sleep enough to be prepared for work. He enjoyed the simplest pleasures with his newfound freedom. Relationships with no commitments, weekend vacations to neighboring islands. Now he felt on top of the world! He knew as long as his heart and mind could bury his dream, hurt and pain would never find its way to his heart ever again. He had attained what most men would only dream of, wine, women and song were all you ever needed was the creed of the generation he grew up in, and now he had attained just that. The happiness he felt, created and given into, was his, and no one could take it from him. Yet even though he was convinced, there seemed to be something hiding in the distance, eluding

him, yet calling to him as a mate would call the other in the

wild, searching, waiting to be found.

<u>Chapter Twenty-Four</u>

"Confrontation"

All day his mind raced, body and soul in torment as the dreadful day would approach with out delay. Even though Christmas was only a few weeks away, his soon to be x-wife refused to stay long enough for them to share it one last time as a family together. Work had been tedious as he tried to redirect his pain into the work at hand. Reluctantly he answered his cell phone and what he heard had almost stopped his beating heart. He knew the voice of the owner of the "Old Drug Store" for many years, as the question came over the earpiece, his friend asked, "Who was this man in his store hugging and kissing your wife?"

Blake asked for a description. He had no way knowing who this person was with his wife. As the description was revealed, his knees felt weak. His stomach now churning, wrenched in disgust at what had been unveiled to him now.

The pain now deep within him, he felt rage as he snapped!

The phone closed to end the call. Overcome, he now recalled

the past several years and questioned what he had dismissed

so easily. He had to be absolutely sure. Quickly he went to

the house. Her car was there as they had gone to town in

a different vehicle. The caller I.D. held several numbers of

recent incoming calls. Several from an area code located in

the buckeye state. A quick check of phone records of past

bills revealed times and dates spanning the entire time since

they had arrived here in the sunshine state.

Confirming his worst nightmare, a living nightmare,

he placed the police revolver in the nap of his back beneath

his shirt. Emotions now running wild, Blake knew he must not

confront them in this state of mind, should they return. He

needed time to think and get control of his pain and anger.

His training from the military as a police officer as well as his father's values would demand control. He needed to vent, and working on the building would accomplish this task. As each grieving hour passed he thought of the entire scenario, when the calls had been made, some even as he slept, not more then twenty feet from her as she talked to his own brother, The Betrayer. He wondered how long it had been going on. But -- most of all he wondered why?

Eleven o'clock, it was late, and his baby girl would be sound asleep by now. The time had come for confrontation. Pulling into the driveway, he recognized the additional vehicle parked there. The betrayer had been his own brother. The same family blood ran thru both their veins. It was incomprehensible to him that a part of his own family would betray him. As he entered thru the front door, he found them in the kitchen drinking wine, with his baby girl awake on the kitchen floor. Control of his rage was difficult but he had to maintain control, had do hear it for himself.

As he instructed his wife to take their child to bed, he instructed his brother to meet him in the master bedroom's bathroom, to confront this betrayer. His anger now was only thwarted by this unthinkable act that his own brother could commit." What in Gods' name do you think you are doing?" were the only words he could find to even attempt to voice the emotions that pounded from the very core of his bones, that held the same bloodline as he who now stood in front of him. His response revealed surprise in his voice as did his question, "What are you talking about?" The Betrayer replied, as if startled by Blake's statement. The revolver pressed into Blake's back beneath his shirt, as if calling, urging him to release it to deliver judgment as if judge and jury had pronounced sentence. The silence of thought was now broken, as his own blood began to boil from the next words uttered from the betrayer's own mouth.

Blake stood in awe as his ears beheld and his mind pondered the words, "Would you not want me to raise your child than some jerk?" His own response came quicker than he could ever think it. From his own lips, he replied with a thundering clash, "NO! You are a jerk!" it seemed, the only reply that would suffice. In his own mind, he knew what he could do and get away with under the mask of a crime of passion. In what seemed a flash of light the thought of taking the lives of these two, would be justified as he reached behind his back for the revolver.

Chapter Twenty-Five

"Lady in red"

With the workweek ended, Blake found himself in the same routine. Now at the club sitting at a table with a friend, she passed right in front of him. With no thought, or time to react in the midst of his conversation, the words came from within him as if passed by an unknown spirit, "Lady in Red," he had said aloud with out knowing it. She had taken his breath away, as well as his conversation that he was obviously not interested in any more. From hair to shoes, she wore red, as he had never witnessed before. It had been well over a year since he had felt the pull from deep within his chest. This he would learn would be no ordinary woman but one who would change his life forever.

"Hey!," came from across the table finally breaking his concentration as he stared, his eyes and head turned to follow this "Lady in Red" across the club floor. It had been many a year since a woman had turned his head and completely caught his attention. His friend now uttered in disbelief, "The great Mr. Lucky losing control?" was his comment as he chuckled like a hyena calling out into the wild. Oh no was Blake's reply, though deep down the assurance was much less than he knew. As the conversation came to a close, Blake knew he had to confront this "Lady in Red." There was a need deep inside as though a part of him knew what the rest of him could not ascertain. The opening advance would be spontaneous, though he always relied on his wit and cleverness to say the right things at the right time. This time would be no different.

As she approached his eyes met hers, and he spoke, "The Lady in Red." It seemed to instantly catch her attention as he spoke it. Almost immediately, Blake sensed a calm and warming demeanor about her from the smile that graced her face. As they began to talk, the words seem to flow as easily as rain from clouds eagerly wanting to reach the earth below. Time passed so quickly, before they both had realized the club had begun to fill with the evening's show of enthusiastic patrons. Some seeking fulfillment and other drowning their sorrows in their own choice of Poison. As they talked, a song of mutual enjoyment came across the speakers and he asked her to dance. She would reveal one of his most enjoyed passions as one of her own. She danced as though they had been partners forever. As the night progressed, he would dance again with her and find, no matter the style, she followed effortlessly, matching his moves as an orchestra in perfect sync with each stroke of the maestro's wand.

His time was near to DJ and before she left, he asked to see her again. This mutual feeling was evident even from the first second they had met. As the night came to a close, Blake checked to be sure he had not lost the precious number he had received from this "Lady in Red." Now home, his mind captivated by the evening he had enjoyed so much, the test of his inner self would have to be faced. The "Escape" had not beckoned for him in a long time. Now in front of the same mirror that had revealed the void to him, and had allowed the "Escape" to consume him, he stared deep into his own reflection. However, only the thickness of a single glass pane, it seemed to reveal depths deep with in his own eyes, to the core of his very soul. He had not had the strength in the past several years to venture a return to this side of his life, as the nightmares had subsided with less frequency as he con-centrated on his daughter and restrained himself from any relationships, in fear of rejection. The mere thought of awak-ening the void he had hidden so deep within his soul was -- unimaginable. Deeply he peered now into the mirror. Deep into his soul as he searched for any remnant of that which would give rise to what he feared most -- The "Escape!"

Chapter Twenty-Six

"Cast out"

The pain now so great so deep within his soul that Blake's heart pounded, in both anguish and hatred combined. Before him now, his only brother who had committed "The Ultimate Betrayal," Blake held his life in his hands. A split second and it would all be over. His anger now fueled by the thought of what he had discovered, no one would condemn him for his actions in this moment of great distress. If they lived, his family would be taken from him. All that he had hoped to attain would cease to exist. Torn now between family and betrayal Blake looked into the eyes of this traitor to their family name. Yet as his grip tightened around the revolver, a feeling deep within him gave way and brought him back to the values his father had instilled within him.

It seemed an eternity, though only seconds had actually passed before he released the grip on the revolver and returned his arm to his side. Hatred coupled with anger now had to be restrained for a brief time, to allow him to clearly make a decision that would affect all that were here, as well as many more who were not. His reasoning though complicated to most, a cold reality told him that only a simple path remained. Blake knew he could not remain part of his precious daughter's life, nor did he retain inside himself the ability to explain at a later date to his daughter, for what he had done. Now in the living room Blake confronted both with the reality and proof, of the unbearable truth he had discovered. Denying all and any past involvement, despite the proof that stared them both in the face, Blake's only comment came now as a last chance for the betrayal to end.

All the family on both sides would despise his brother, the elder of the children. He would never be allowed to attend family functions, as Blake would see to that enforcement.

Protesting still, Blake in total disbelief, resorted to his fathers'

teaching of Jewish times in the old ways, and tore a piece

of his clothing signifying the death of a family member. He

explained the significance even though they were not Jewish.

The explanation was a simple one. To Blake his brother had

died, at this very moment, and that he would never forget let

alone forgive the path his brother had chosen. His brothers

response again, even though educated with a degree, was

that of a mere shallow minded entity with out the ability to

foresee the ramifications of what his actions would collater-

ally bring upon all who were related.

Now, witnessing the loss of his own brother, Blake

cast him out, with instructions never to show his face to him

again for he would not acknowledge him as anyone other then

a stranger. Turning to his adulterous wife, he announced with

conviction that the divorce papers would now be changed.

To continue this vile relationship she would give up all interest in the assets they owned, or he would re-file for divorce under adultery. The pain deep inside his soul now began to register what was beginning to unveil before him, and all he had striven for, all he had attained, wife, daughter, family and life as he knew it, would soon be divided by what he could only condemn as – "The Ultimate Betrayal." "For with in those closest to you, deception and deceit transforms the innocent into the **guilty!**"

Chapter Twenty-Seven

"The past revealed"

His life was shattered now, into shards as that of a pane of glass obliterated by the impact of a young boy's baseball gone astray. She would even deny him now, the two additional weeks before leaving, of a final family Christmas together with his daughter. The pain of this loss was great and heavy on his soul. Blake knew not if he could bare it as he kissed his precious daughter goodbye, he watched in disbelief, as his family he held so dear, seemed to take with them all of whom he was, all he had become and ever would be. With the betrayer at the wheel the dagger became sharper than any two edged sword, forged in the bowels of hell itself, by the master of its domain. It now pierced thru and breached all that he had faith in and held true and dear.

Christmas day had arrived carrying a bleakness shrouded by the absence of the joys it always brought. A single phone call would throw him into utter confusion and bring out the depth of what the betrayer had done. For this phone call, on the day celebrating our Lord's birth, would reveal many truths and it would crush the very foundation of his belief in a sovereign entity. For revealed to him were dates, times and years of this vile affair which went far beyond the mere four years he was aware it had covered, but a decade, even before he had known his wife to be. Substantiated by the betrayers' first wife, the nurse, the identity of this affair had been one in the same. As the voice on the other end of the phone continued Blake's knees began to fail and buckle beneath him, he listened, as the voice revealed identical plane flights of returns to the lone star state, from both the sunshine and buckeye states. As the confusion started to clear he remembered past events, signs that he had missed.

For he had been blinded by his devotion and profound commitment to both love and passion for his beloved wife.

Now as he sunk deeper into a state of loss and realization, he began to wonder how long ago this person had known about these facts. Yet most of all he was more concerned with why they had chosen not reveal this information that had become so destructive, and why was it to be revealed at this time of ultimate chaos. With the phone now on the hook, Blake realized comparing past events with what had just been revealed to him now, that this person had knowledge of these events from past times. As easily as a child fits pegs into the shapes that match, it was not hard for Blake to add up all the signs and deceptions. For she had become best friends with his wife long ago, and became as close to each other as friends could be. She knew of the affair with Blake's wife before they were married, which had started during the betrayers' first marriage, second marriage and ongoing relationships, even after Blake had married her.

This dagger that the betrayer had buried deep in his heart and soul, burned with a fire so fierce he was barely able to control what emotions he had but held onto. When now deep within his wound, he felt the dagger twist as if to insinuate, "this pain had only yet begun." For he realized now! There had been a third member to his family's demise. Who knew, yet refused to come forward, the elder of his two younger siblings had gripped the dagger within him and twisted his very soul apart.

Chapter Twenty-Eight

"The Birth of Deception"

Separated now from, body, soul and mind, Blake pondered the last decade of events, combined with the information received by the elder of his two siblings. As this puzzle in life began to take shape, he remembered from the betrayer's New Years Eve party where he had seen her before. At their business together. Where she always arrived around lunchtime. She would leave her vehicle for Blake to repair or be serviced. The betrayer would take her back to work, returning much later, requesting details to what had been the problem with her vehicle. When going for parts he would leave during lunch and not return for many hours. Hours were spent as well at a gym in a near by city which would reveal where she worked part time. Yet New Years Eve when they had met was no coincidence, Blake had learned she had asked his brother to leave his wife and be with her. He constantly declined her proposition.

Blake's homecoming with his brother found no reconciliation, and she, infuriated with his brother's refusal to leave his family, found both Blake and his brother's mistress in the office to use the phone. This, Blake now feared, was when the deception had begun. He, unaware then to what had conspired, innocently responded to her pondering questions and agreed to remain at the New Years Eve gathering. If only he had known. He had fallen for her then, as a knight from King Arthur's realm had once fallen for his own Guinevere. Then life as he knew it would have been very different. Now as his own brother watched his mistress, dancing and enjoying the company of his own younger sibling, he neither approached nor warned of their relationship together. Even as time passed, as light from a distant star travels a long journey, silently among all with out drawing attention. Therefore, this relationship was built upon lies and deception, only with a sadistic ulterior motive and intent.

Blake now enveloped by the very thought of this woman, would bring her into the fold of his family. The wedding would be planned, and Blake's own father would attend the first of his children's weddings. This in itself was one of the greatest honors his father would bestow upon him. Blake honored his father above all. For he had only wanted since he was young, to make his father proud of him, and receive his father's blessing. The wedding would be one of a kind that all would remember. With his eldest of the younger sisters at the piano, Blake sang to his bride. Both sides of the family had attended in full, including his father. Blake's nephew and niece were part of this sacred wedding, as well as his own brother, ironically his own brother was best man. As the preacher announced, "Is there, anyone here who knows why these two should not be joined in holy matrimony, speak now or forever hold your peace." Blake's own best man, his blood brother and now betrayer, would not utter a single word of protest let alone remorse, as his mistress, not ten feet from him silent as well, would now be joined with his younger sibling.

With vows sealed by the words, "I pronounce you man and wife," this couple turned to a church full of friends and family to start their new lives together. As the music played, they passed each row of people with smiles and happiness upon the faces of all there. All too soon, Blake would learn another family member present at the wedding would discover the adulterous relationship with the best man and bride to be. They too would also keep their discovery as silent as the tomb of Egypt's own pharaoh's, that held deep their silent secrets that would destroy an empire, only to be revealed later when discovered by those who seek the unanswered questions. Forced now to reveal the truth after years of guilt held deep inside, Blake would learn the true meaning of, "Family Intent."

Chapter Twenty-Nine

"Depth of the Dagger"

The summer brought with it the warmth of the sun and the prospect of the annual summer vacation trip to God's own country to see his parents. Blake always enjoyed the drive up as his daughter and he would play several road games for hours on end. This particular trip was no different with the exception of how much his daughter had grown. However, barely a decade old now, her mannerisms and intelligence were easily that of a teenager. Each summer when his daughter flew out, Blake would visit his parents. These were the only times his parents would get to see their grand child. The drive was long yet the hours passed by as though it were a simple drive in the park. As father and daughter played and talked the hours away, catching up since their last visit.

As they pulled into the driveway, his mother was always waiting to greet them as if a long lost child had just been found and returned. These were special times for Blake. He and his father would work or talk together far into the evening. Religion would always top the conversation each year and Blake would sit and listen to his father's words for hours on end. Each story his father would tell captivated him as a child listening to story time. Each year many of the same stories would be told. Some returned several times in the same week due to his father's age, and some even repeated in the same evening. He cherished his father's stories and each year a new one, old and forgotten, would surface to encompass yet another page in the family's history.

This year would be somewhat different from previous summers. The betrayer had finally married Blake's ex-wife eight years later. Many times he and his father talked far into the morning hours. The subject this year would begin with the usual stories and discussions. However, these would fall far short of Blake's amusement to what his father would soon reveal. The evening began with the usual religious and family stories. Yet soon his father turned to stories of the past family business. Blake listened with eyes and ears poised like a dog on point, alerted by movement in a field of maze. What was to be revealed would startle his soul with such a force that he himself would have a difficult time accepting the words that his father uttered.

As he listened, his father began the story of all stories. Blake had not known a great deal about his ex-wife's past only that she had married once before. He accepted her as of the day they met and held no longing to delve into her past. Yet now as the words came from the man Blake most respected and trusted, he knew these words and stories were true. As his father continued, he recognized several stories about the business and several he had not known. As Blake had guessed his brother, would inevitably loose the business due to failure of actually being there to run it. As his father's stories continued, Blake was mesmerized as a child witnessing their first meteor shower cascading across the heavens. Tales he knew all too well of his brother's promiscuous endeavors. Yet there seemed to be something different, as the words that were spoken next seemed to hang on the edge of reality itself, waiting to cross over from a distant and unknown world. Blake was unprepared for what was about to take place let alone what would follow.

"If only I had known a little bit sooner" his father sighed, "I could have saved you from all this". He wondered what his father had meant and now his curiosity would be squelched, as quickly as it had been peaked. As Blake listened intently, his father continued to reveal what Blake had not known for over a decade and a half. His father had discovered shortly after the wedding that the woman who had just married his youngest son, and the woman who had the

affair with his eldest son, were both one and the same! The

dagger that Blake's brother had thrust into his very soul, and

his eldest of two sisters that had twisted it to thresholds of pain

unknown, as intense as the fires that burn in hell itself, would

now be ripped from deep within him -- by his own father.

<u>Chapter Thirty</u>

"The Reckoning"

Though Blake was certain his father acted with no malicious intent, yet in his own way, it seemed he was trying to comfort -- no to help bear the pain, and sorrow he felt emanating from his youngest son. Like his father before him, Blake's father was a simple man, endowed with wisdom and common sense that would rival the ancient prophets of old. A good man, well respected and honored. Even now, Blake listened, as his father revealed all that he knew, it was as if before the world had been created, and time had stood still, more over time seemed to, not exist at all.

Before he knew it, hours had passed quicker than a flicker of light thru the expanse of the known universe. Blake now had realized his father, in his own way had been apologizing the entire time. He had held the secrets within him and now revealed to his son with a level of emotion he had never

seen from his father. Blake realized now that his father held

himself somewhat responsible and it was now up to Blake

to right the wrong his father had put upon himself. As they

talked, Blake reassured his father regardless of what had

happened and even if he had told him sooner, that his love for

his wife and dedication to family would still have blinded him.

For even at the least he would have not accepted as truth

what his father would have told him, for he was in love.

As a gentle rain blankets and comforts mother earth

herself, Blake could feel and see the burden that had just

been lifted from his father's soul. Yet with out even knowing

until this very moment, his father had revealed more than just

past events. Now stunned as if all the blood that ran thru his

body had suddenly stopped flowing only to be released again

all at a single moment, his father had done what no other

could have done. Blake had accepted that his nightmares and

constant torments at the loss of his family would never end.

Yet in his father's words were not where he gained this knowl-

edge, but from the release of the burden that his father had

carried. In this, Blake found what he had searched for since

the loss of his family, and the emergence of the "Escape".

Even now as he watched and listened to his father's

tones and mannerisms, Blake became aware of his own

burden that he had put upon himself, holding it in place

much like his father had done to himself for all these years.

Allowing his past to consume his present he now understood

that without the same release of responsibility for what had

happened, he too would continue to suffer as his father had

done, by carrying over his loss into his own future. As if

coming out of a coma from years of reliving the same sce-

nario, he knew now what had to be done. The darkness in

his very soul would have to be dealt with. He must find a way

to forgive himself. The "Escape" was not his ally, nor was it a place where none could hurt or destroy him. However, it was a prison within his own psyche that was there only when it needed to take control. Now he realized it was always there, controlling, never allowing him to live outside the prison that had captured the very persona of who he was.

His father unaware of the gift he had just given his son now continued with joyful stories of his past life and childhood. His father seemed to tell the stories in a different light and tone that Blake remembered from long ago. As the year's visit came to a close, Blake knew what waited ahead. The drive home would not seem as long this trip, as his thoughts were now focused, on what lie seemingly dormant like a "wolf in sheep's clothing" waiting for him at home. The "Escape" must be beckoned! once again. Now more than ever he needed it, yearned for it. For it was part of him. A part that he had to confront now on his terms. Face to face. For now he new what it was and how to defeat it. The strength, courage and power were to come from one place alone. His father had shown him where the key had been all along. As Blake had released his father from his prison, so would he now release himself. The "Escape" may have locked him away, but the bond of love between a father and a daughter was the key that could open any lock. Blake's own daughter would set him free, for within her he found himself. As within him, all that his father had become was found within himself. That same bond between father and son that Blake so cherished, was how his father had opened his eyes and pointed the way. Now as Blake stood before the mirror, the floor yielded not its cold grip that once had held him. His eyes were not dark and void, but now baby blue as his daughters at birth. The loss of his daughter once claimed his very soul in this spot. Now with the hope and love of this same daughter, within himself and his daughter apart of him, they could face the "Escape" together.

<u>Chapter Thirty-One</u>

"The Home Coming"

Deeply he stared into the endless depths. Where mirror images ended and what lie deep within began. Years had passed by since he had gained the courage to face what had been dormant within his psyche. Now he searched for it, to be absolutely sure it would never return. Never to reclaim what was his again. His essence and soul were his now, and before he could give himself one final time to be with someone forever, he must be secure in the fact that the "Void" had been filled and the "Escape" would not come for him now, or hereafter. Deeper and deeper Blake searched now as he focused intensely within a place far beyond the confines and reflections of the mirror that hung before him. This would be the first of three tests to determine if the recovery had both begun, and continued to heal the wound that had been inflicted with such malicious intent! Deeper still he searched, yet he found not as much as a hint of the "Void" that would beckon the "Escape". The "Void" had been both healed and filled, by the constant support and care of family and friends. Moreover, the hope and dream of his daughters return. Blake moved into the living room in front of the Television where the video tape had been previously loaded. The click of the remote gave way to the sound of the video recorder playing the current selection. The second test had begun. As the figures of his x-wife, daughter and past family surroundings flashed across the screen, a simple smile arose upon his face as he relished the joy of memories embedded within him of a time not so long ago. Depression and heavy heartedness would not find him now. As the hours and tapes went by, Blake felt a sense of existence in his daughter's life, as well as a part in their ever-changing future together. Joy and happiness at what he had helped to bring into this world as part of his family, neither was tarnished by past events, nor would be in future times.

The final proving would be revealed only from deep within his subconscious. Would the nightmares continue and not relinquish there hold on his psyche? or would the love of his daughters future return be enough to vanquish the "Escape" forever. Now as he lay fixated on nothing specific above him, Blake imagined what it would be like when his daughter would return with eyes wide opened to the events of the past. How old would she be? Moreover, would she understand what had come to pass? He often recalled his precious daughter bursting through the line at the airport as she had done so many times when she was younger. Now as he imagined his daughter as a young adult with the same exhilarated smile upon her face, emerging through the bustle of people exiting the aircraft, he heard the familiar sound of the words he longed to hear. "Daddy! Daddy!"

The flight was long and the suspense was even greater. However, she new the secrecy and surprise would far outweigh the tedious move. As the flight seemed to go on forever, she read again to herself the "Letter of acceptance" from the Veterinary College in The Sunshine State. A two fold surprise that she would spring on her unsuspecting father. As she peeked in and saw him sleeping, his daughter paused before waking her father. She had never seen him sleep so peaceably and contently in all the years she had known him. The smile on his face was one of a loving father at peace and rest with his inner self. Blake had fallen asleep, and yet in this dream he would dream a new dream! For as his daughter softly whispered in his ear to awaken him, "Daddy!, Daddy!" his dream would become a reality. The "Escape" had been vanquished by the love and hope between a father and daughter. So strong that none could keep apart. They were together again.

"*Daddy's little girl had come home*".

About the Author

Randolph Blake was raised on the outskirts of Cleveland Ohio. As his father before him, Blake enjoys his gift of being a "Jack of all trades". Currently still enjoying his quest to experience Life to it's fullest as well as to fuel his "sponge for knowledge", Blake continues with his first love --Music. As an accomplished musician having shared the stage from Blues to Classic Rock, and embracing the thrill of being a private DJ.

Blake's zest for life is only matched by his love for his only daughter. Blake currently residing in the Sunshine State employed in Law Enforcement, looks forward each day to the new and exciting experiences that life itself can bring thru the

vast inexperianced resources --that the World has to offer.

-- Live Life for the moment.

For the next may never come.